THE DOMINIE WORLD OF INV

MW01174476

INTRODUCING ARTHROPODS

Written by Graham Meadows & Claire Vial

CONTENTS

Dominie Press, Inc.

THE ARTHROPODS

Arthropods make up more than 80 percent of all known animal **species**. They are found in almost all **habitats**, ranging from deserts to the deep sea.

Most arthropods have a hard outer skeleton, called an exoskeleton. The exoskeleton is made of a substance called chitin. Chitin can be hard, as in the cutting edges of claws or jaws, or softer and more flexible, as in the hinges linking body segments.

An exoskeleton cannot expand. Most arthropods must shed their exoskeleton from time to time in order to grow. This shedding process is called molting.

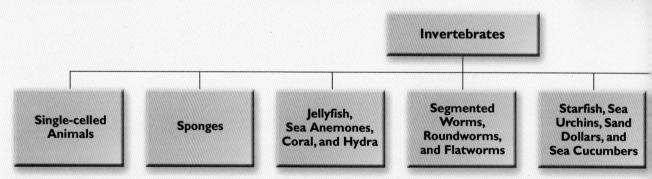

(Note: This chart does not show all the groups of invertebrates.)

Freshwater Crayfish ▲

Earwig ▶

Mollusks Slugs & Snails, Shellfish, Octopuses, and Squid	Arthropods	
Crustaceans Crabs, Lobsters, and Relatives	Arachnids Spiders, Scorpions, and Relatives	Centipedes, Millipedes, and Insects

Purple Rock Crab ▲

CRUSTACEANS

Crabs, lobsters, and their relatives are called crustaceans. Most crustaceans are marine animals. Some live in fresh water, and a few live on land.

Their bodies have three parts: the head, the thorax, and the abdomen. The head has two pairs of **antennae** and one pair of eyes. In many crustaceans, the eyes are on the end of **stalks**, or long, thin strands that support the eyes.

Most species have between six and fourteen pairs of limbs. Some of these limbs are used for walking; others are used for swimming. Some species have one pair of limbs shaped into **pincers**, or claws.

In many types of crustaceans, a hard shell, called a carapace, covers the head and thorax.

Most crustaceans are **omnivores**. Their **diet** includes both plants and other animals.

Hermit Crab ▶

5

Marine Crustaceans

Lobsters and crabs have five pairs of limbs. Four pairs are used for walking or swimming. The front pair has large claws shaped into pincers.

Crabs usually move sideways, but they can move in any direction.

Shrimp swim rather than crawl. They have five pairs of walking legs and five pairs of swimming legs.

Krill are tiny, shrimp-like crustaceans that are eaten by certain types of whales.

Barnacles attach themselves to objects such as wharves, boats, and rocks.

Sand hoppers, also called beach fleas, are not really fleas. They are small crustaceans that live in sand.

Rock lobsters, also called crayfish, do not have pincers.

◀ Barnacles

▲ **Common Rock Pool Shrimp**

Inland Saltwater Crustaceans

Brine shrimp live only in inland saltwater lakes. They are not found in oceans. They are commonly used as fish food in aquariums.

Freshwater Crustaceans

Freshwater crustaceans include daphnia, also called water fleas, and fairy shrimp, which swim upside down.

Freshwater crayfish, also called crawfish, live in ponds and streams.

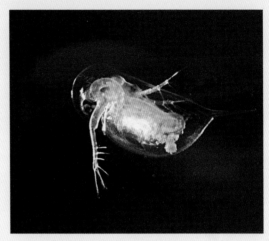

▲ **Daphnia, or Water Flea**

Land Crustaceans

Woodlice, also called sow bugs, pill bugs, or slaters, live in damp places. When they are alarmed, some species can roll into a ball.

Land hoppers live in damp places such as under rotting logs. They are related to sand hoppers.

Slater, or Pill Bug ▶

▲ Freshwater Crayfish

Scorpion ▲

Orb Web Spider ▶

ARACHNIDS

Spiders, scorpions, and their relatives are called arachnids. They have four pairs of walking legs. Arachnids have no antennae and no wings. Most are **carnivores** that live alone.

▲ **Green Orb Spider**

A spider's body has two parts: a head connected to a thorax, and an abdomen. Spiders have special glands that produce silk. Most types of spiders have six or eight eyes. They have a pair of jaws equipped with hollow fangs through which **venom** can be injected into their **prey**.

Most spiders feed on insects.

A scorpion's body has three parts. Scorpions have a pair of large pincers. Most have a long tail with a poisonous stinger at the end. The stinger is used to **paralyze** their prey. Most types of scorpions are **nocturnal**.

Harvestmen are closely related to mites and ticks. They have only one part to their body, and only two eyes. They do not produce silk and have no fangs. Instead, they have special stink glands that they use for defense.

Most mites are too small to be seen with the human eye. They are found in many kinds of habitats.

Ticks have a tough, round body. All ticks are **parasites**. They feed on the blood of animals such as sheep, cattle, and birds. Some ticks also feed on humans.

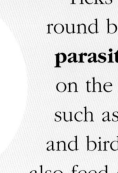

▲ **Cattle Tick**

Ticks spread many diseases.

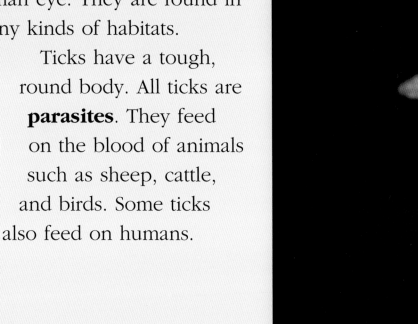

▲ **Harvestman**

Giant Centipede ▲

House Centipede ▶

CENTIPEDES AND MILLIPEDES

Centipedes and millipedes have long bodies made up of segments. Their body length ranges from less than one inch to eleven inches. Most centipedes and millipedes are nocturnal.

Centipedes have a flat body with one pair of legs on each segment. All centipedes are carnivores. Their diet includes insects, earthworms, and other invertebrates. They bite their prey and inject venom into it.

Millipedes have a circular body with two pairs of legs on each segment. They do not have a poisonous bite. Most millipedes feed on dead plants. When they are threatened, they often curl up into a ball. Some millipedes have special stink glands that give off a bad smell to drive off **predators**.

Millipede ▲

INSECTS

Insects are the most successful group of animals ever to exist on Earth. There are more than a million known species of insects, and many scientists believe there could be 15 to 30 million more species still to be discovered. Insects are found in almost every type of environment, except the sea.

Insect Classification

Scientists classify insects into different groups. Some of these groups are:

- Dragonflies and damselflies
- Mantids
- Cockroaches
- Termites
- Earwigs
- Grasshoppers, locusts, crickets, and katydids
- Stick insects
- Lice
- Bugs (cicadas and aphids, for example)
- Beetles
- Fleas
- Flies, mosquitoes, and gnats
- Butterflies and moths
- Bees, wasps, and ants

◀ **Dragonfly**

▼ **Katydid**

Giant Weta ▲

Praying Mantis ▶

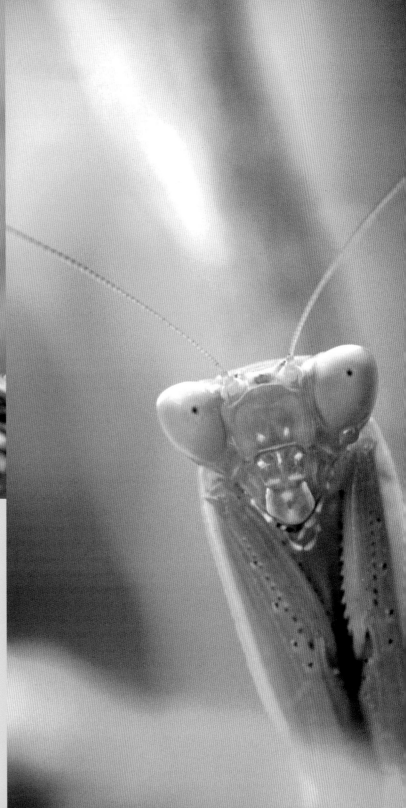

Insect Anatomy

An insect's body is divided into three parts: the head, the thorax, and the abdomen. Insects, such as the praying mantis, have three pairs of legs and a pair of antennae.

Most types of insects have two pairs of wings. Some insects, such as flies, have only one pair of wings. Others, such as stick insects and fleas, do not have wings.

▼ **Common Housefly**

Insects are the only invertebrates that can fly. The study of insects is called entomology.

The giant weta of New Zealand is one of the heaviest insects on Earth. It can weigh up to two and a half ounces.

ARTHROPODS AND THEIR IMPORTANCE TO HUMANS

How They Are Useful

- Arthropods play an important part in the **food chain**. They break down plant and animal material and are food for many other animals.

- Humans eat many types of arthropods, such as shellfish and lobsters.

- Some arthropods help to control other invertebrates that are pests. For example, ladybugs eat aphids, which often damage plants.

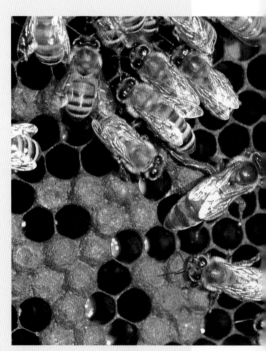

- Some insects produce food that we can eat. For example, honeybees produce honey.

- Some arthropods produce materials that are useful to humans. Examples include beeswax and silk.

Honeybees Producing Honey ▶

▲ **Bower Bird Eating a Grub**

Locust ▲

How They Are Harmful

- Many arthropods are pests. Some, such as slugs and locusts, eat crops that people grow for food.

- Others, such as ants and cockroaches, can be pests inside people's homes.

- Flies that land on our food can spread germs.

- Some arthropods, including termites and beetle larvae, **bore** into and destroy wooden structures, such as buildings and decks.

- Ticks and mosquitoes feed on blood, and they can spread diseases.

- Some arthropods, such as scorpions and some spiders, are poisonous to humans.

- Wasps and bees can inflict painful stings.

- The redback spider of Australia can give a painful bite.

▲ **Redback Spider**

GLOSSARY

antennae: Thin, movable parts of an insect's head that help it to sense its surroundings

bore: To make a hole in something

carnivores: Animals that eat other animals

diet: The food that an animal or a person usually eats

food chain: A term used to describe how all living things, predators and prey, feed on other living things in order to survive

habitats: Areas where animals and plants live and grow

nocturnal: Active at night

omnivores: Animals that eat both plants and other animals

paralyze: To make an animal unable to move

parasites: Animals that live on other animals and use them to survive

pincers: Front claws used for holding on to things

predators: Animals that hunt, catch, and eat other animals

prey: Animals that are hunted and eaten by other animals

species: Types of animals that have some physical characteristics in common

stalks: Long, thin strands that support an animal's eyes

venom: Deadly poison

INDEX